How to D Angry Temperam

GU00836384

...uus

Understand Why Kids are Angry and Learn the Ways to Manage Their Anger and Temperament

By:

Claire Stranberg

Get an Awesome Gift Right Now!

Get your FREE GIFT NOW by going to

http://www.mritchi.com/free-ebooks/

As a way of saying thanks for your purchase, I'm offering these 2 books for FREE exclusive to my readers.

Also, you'll be the first to GET an instant access to FREE giveaways and freebies EXCLUSIVE to our SUBSCRIBERS only.

Get your FREE GIFT NOW by going to

http://www.mritchi.com/free-ebooks/

ISBN-13: 978-1508914037

ISBN-10: 1508914036

https://www.amazon.com/author/clairestranberg

Contents

Introduction

How do you handle your kids' constant temper tantrums? Do you get frustrated, mystified and end up being angry yourself? Do you panic and rush in to solve your child's problem immediately or do you get caught up in power struggles? Don't you just wish you could stay composed and rational through all your young child's outbursts of anger?

Dealing with your kids' fits of anger is one of the many challenges and stressful situations you will face as a parent and sometimes you might be unsure if you're doing the right thing. The good news is that you learn as you go. Besides slipping into a fight with your kids, there are realistic and effective ways you can do to triumph over this challenge. Your kids' temper flare ups don't mean you're a failure as a parent, it means that something needs changing.

When confronted with a child's angry behavior, it is important not to take it as a personal attack on you. Your best defense is to understand the circumstances that cause your child to blow a fuse and to prepare yourself for such situations. It pays to have compassion even though you feel like you're at your wits end.

Triggers are different in every child. Sometimes it may need a little hard work to discover the events, thoughts and feelings that precede your kid's anger. By being able to identify and address this anger, you can better help them cope with challenges. You can prevent serious problems that develop if kids don't learn to express their anger in healthy ways.

In this book, we will explore several factors that usually stir up anger in kids, strategies you can use to deal with their angry outbursts and ways you can guide their expressions of anger.

We will also look at different temperament types that can give you helpful insights into what makes your child tick. By taking into consideration that your child's behavior is a result of both his natural inclination and his environment, you can find ways of teaching your kids how to control angry impulses and enhance his overall well-being without changing who he is.

Chapter 1: Uncovering the Causes of Anger in Kids

Dealing with children's anger can be puzzling and exhausting. Some parents are filled with embarrassment when their kids display unsettling anger outbursts often for no apparent reason. Yet, there certainly are reasons.

Most of the time, your kids' angry and aggressive behavior push your own angry button, but that's okay because it compels you to fix the problem. You want your kids' behavior corrected and you don't want how it triggers angry feelings in you.

Instead of lashing out at your kids and give in to power struggle, it is important to operate from a place of understanding. This not only increases your tolerance but more importantly, it enables you to teach your kids to master this powerful and complex emotion.

Awareness is the first step to understanding why your kids lose it. One of the biggest mistakes you can make when dealing with a child's angry behavior is creating solutions without understanding the root cause. By having a clear picture of the causes of angry impulses in kids, you can protect them from violent outbursts and help them get a grip of their anger. You can take these behaviors as good opportunities to help your kids learn about self control.

It is important to remember that anger is not the same thing as aggression. Anger is a feeling, while aggression is a behavior. Feeling angry is okay, hurting another person or destroying property is not. Your goal is not to destroy or repress anger in your kids or in yourself but to manage it in healthy and appropriate ways.

Anger is not necessarily a bad emotion. Actually, it sometimes helps a person reach his goals or get what he wants in life by leading him to do a spontaneous action. It could also provide enough courage to stimulate someone to begin something that he is holding back for a long time.

Mentally, anger is a driving or motivating force. Have you noticed that when you want something really bad, the motivation to get it becomes higher when you are angry? The same is true for kids. So understanding how the emotion of anger works can help you a lot in trying to deal with your child's temper tantrums. Being angry can be helpful, but how you and your kid will respond to that feeling is what you are trying to manage.

The thing to realize is that anger is a universal reaction to pain. It is normal for children to have episodes of angry outbursts and fighting with other children. Unable to understand and verbalize their frustration in certain situations, kids act out in anger. It can be triggered by loneliness, anxiety, embarrassment and hurt.

To prevent serious problems that develop if children do not learn how to control their angry impulses, you have to get a clear picture of the full range of factors that influence your child's temperamental behavior

Physical discomfort

First, you need to find out if there are biological factors contributing to your child's outbursts. Maybe your child is allergic to dust, pollen or some food and cause him much discomfort. Maybe some ear infection is causing him pain or maybe he finds it difficult to fall asleep or stay asleep throughout the night. Your moods can change too when you're sick.

Anger is an instinctive reaction to pain. It is a natural human response to get angry when you are hurt or when something physically bothers you. Anger is commonly accompanied by what is so-called the "fight-or-flight response", which induces a person to defend himself automatically.

When you notice that your child seems to be angry all the time, you may want to consider the possibility of any physical discomfort, sickness, or condition. Do not hesitate to consult a healthcare professional regarding it.

Life challenges

After ruling out biological factors, figure out other life stressors that may be triggering your kids' anger. Is your child expected to perform beyond his capabilities? Does he feel frustrated because of low academic performance? Identify unsolved problems and lacking skills that cause your child to lose control. Many of the kids who exhibit angry behavior are simply lacking the skills to do the tasks demanded of them. Find out why your child is not doing well on an activity. Knowing your kids, their skills, the demands being put on them allow you to give the kind of support they need to cope with stressful situations.

Another thing that may trigger your child's anger is the inability to cope with certain situations that are happening in his or her life. Some of them are quite significant, and are discussed in detail below, such as coping with parents' divorce or marital problems and experiencing rejection from friends. Other seemingly small circumstances, like their inability to properly sharpen a pencil or refill their own water bottle at school, can cause frustrations that could also lead to anger outbursts.

There are many ways on how to help children develop their self-esteem, and to teach them how to cope with changes, disappointments and frustrations. You could make a quick research about it online or you can consult a child psychologist as well.

Parental actions

Some kids have anger problems as a result of modeling after a parent's excessive expression of anger. Are you unconsciously transmitting anger to your child? Are you overly critical or overprotective? You need be aware of your own behavior that may be harming your child's sense of self worth.

You should realize that as a parent, everything that your child would copy or imitate would all start with you. You are your child's number one role model, and you should start acting that way. If you get angry at the smallest amount of agitation, then you may have anger management problems. Try considering professional help or therapy to improve your condition.

Talk to your spouse about how both of your actions and behaviors affect your child's temper. Avoid quarrelling in front of your child as much as you can. When you have something to argue about, do it inside a room without the presence of anyone else. If you will learn how to handle your own anger, then it is more likely that your children could follow suit.

Marital discord

When parents fight, they spill over negative emotions to their children. Witnessing bitter and ongoing conflict between parents compounds children's anger and can destroy children's internal unity and security.

Whether you like it or not, your child gets a significant amount of his or her sense of security from your relationship with your spouse. When it is compromised, your child could develop frequent anger frenzies that will most probably lead to aggressive behavior in the home and at school. Teachers may have a hard time disciplining him or her, not knowing that the root cause of his outbursts is his parents' marital problems.

It is really amazing how kids can feel and discern if their mom and dad are happy and getting along with each other well. A good marriage relationship results to a happier and more peaceful home, especially for the children.

Peer Rejection

Anger can result from rejection by peers. Children crave acceptance to develop a healthy self-esteem. You need to be aware of the many ways this rejection can manifest on your child including isolation, hostility toward others and social anxiety.

You cannot really do anything when it comes to the actions of other kids towards your child. You cannot control what these others kids will do or how they would interact with your child. In order to lessen the effects of peer rejection, you need to help your child build up his or her own self-esteem and it all starts at home.

How you treat each other within the family – from the father, mother, and siblings – makes or breaks the self-confidence of your children. Be sure to encourage support, sympathy, kindness, cooperation, compassion and courtesy among your children. Of course, you and your spouse should emulate the same values. If they can find these things in your own home, then they would not look for it from their peers outside the home.

Temperament

Your child's challenging behavior may be rooted to his natural dispositions and tendencies. You have to be aware of your child's temperament and respect his uniqueness.

Aside from your child's natural temperament or personality, his frequent anger surges may also be caused by neurodevelopmental disorders such as bipolar disorder, attention deficit hyperactivity disorder (ADHD), or other learning disabilities. When a child suffers from one of these conditions, his feelings of helplessness and incompetence could cause him to become angry with himself and this anger upon himself can easily manifest in also getting angry at all of those around him.

Diet

Certain studies claim that a child's diet could also affect his or her temperament. Experts have observed that the kinds of food a person eats is related to his mood and disposition. If one is not eating enough healthy and nourishing foods and tends to eat more sweets, fatty and processed foods, then it can lead to a more aggressive behavior. This finding is also true when it comes to children.

Processed foods, especially those that are rich in chemicals and other additives, are said to induce anger and destructive behavior in toddlers and school-age kids. A diet composed of more natural and organic foods have shown to affect a significant improvement in mood and temperament among kids.

Identify and Address the Cause of Anger

Failure to identify and address the cause of anger has serious consequences to your child's mental and emotional health and his relationships with other people. By expressing interest in your kids' activities and being responsive to anger-triggering situations, it will be easier to find out what they feel and work through their feelings.

A child finds security from his strong attachments to parents, friends and relatives. It is important to pay attention to children when they are looking for love and affection. You should be motivated by the need to protect and to reach out. Anger in children is often a cry for love and understanding.

The key takeaway? Take your kids' angry outbursts as a signal to fix the cause. You'd be surprised at how delightful your kids can be to be around.

Chapter 2: What Kids Learn by Imitating Their Parents

Parents are the strongest role models for kids. Who you are as a parent shapes your kids' identity and personality development. Your children daily absorb your overt and subtle behaviours, attitudes, mannerisms and expressions.

Where there's constant yelling, shutting people down and fighting for the right to be heard in a family, it's not surprising when kids try what they see and hear at home in the classroom and the playground.

Modelling appropriate behaviour when angry is a powerful tool that you as a parent have in influencing your kids to control angry impulses.

If the child always sees an angry face and hears an angry voice, that's the way he's likely to react when life lets him down. Remember that your kids learn by imitation and he will copy you when it comes to expressing his own anger.

It's challenging when your kids' explosion stirs angry feelings within you. It's natural to get angry but this should not prevent you from responding to your child in a loving, understanding and constructive manner. How do you do it?

Communicate to your child only after you have dealt with your angry feelings.

A parent's immediate expression of anger toward a child can trigger a number of emotional responses in the child including guilt, fear, shame, anxiety and intense anger.

It is important not to give in quickly to the expression of anger. Instead, try to reflect inwardly. This way, you are more careful not to humiliate or shame your kids when giving a correction.

When your kids are not threatened by your expression of anger, they will feel safe and are more receptive to the lessons you are trying to teach.

Identify what triggers you to be angry towards your children and try to be aware whenever these triggers are taking place. Be mindful of these triggers and quietly prepare yourself mentally and emotionally as it comes.

Instead of resisting the anger, allow yourself to feel it. Resisting will only accumulate the rage in your emotions. The important thing is to pause first and reflect about your anger before reacting and talking to your child. What caused you to get angry? Where are you and your child when it happened? What is the weather? What are the circumstances? These questions will help you calm down and act appropriately.

Identify problems that are contributing to your anger.

Are there unresolved hurts in your past that you haven't got over from? Take steps to heal yourself so you can better model emotional health. Also identify present situations that fuel your anger like dissatisfaction with job, frustration with spouse, or financial issues.

Keep in mind that at a young age, your children don't usually understand that your anger isn't about them at all. The danger is that kids often take it personally. They will feel that mom or dad is always angry and doesn't love them.

If you feel that you and your spouse cannot control your own anger or temperament, then it is not shameful to ask for professional help. You may need a psychologist, psychiatrist, or any mental health expert to help you with inner healing or anger management. It is totally acceptable to seek counsel and guidance regarding these matters. Remember that above all you are doing this for the future of your kids.

Be mindful of how you talk to your child.

If you try to teach your kids to do the right thing but are overly critical of them, they are likely to develop fear and insecurity from being constantly judged. They are likely to be angry for not being able to meet unrealistic standards demanded of them.

Instead of criticizing and chastising, try to give them comforting and encouraging words. Let them know that nobody is supposed to be perfect, that everybody commits mistakes (even mom and dad), and there is always a next opportunity to do things better. Teach your children how mistakes or failures could help them learn some lessons that will make them perform better next time. You can say, "You did a nice job at this, but next time it would be better if..."

This way, your child will not only learn how to deal with his or her frustrations, but will build self-esteem and learn perseverance and excellence as well.

Resist the urge to overprotect.

Parents definitely mean well when they overprotect their kids but even loving parents can make children a prisoner of their own home without being aware of doing so. If you smother your kids, repeatedly question their judgment and never trust them to do things on their own, you are inviting resentment.

Children are programmed to explore as much as they possibly can. Being forced to hold back their pure unadulterated need for exploration prevents the kids from developing confidence, having fun and handling situations on their own.

Remember that one of the things that kids explode about is not being able to solve problems. Overprotected children are not given the chance to master problem solving skills. So, ask yourself if your fears, worries and desire to make your child's life stress-free are stifling your kid's happiness and growth.

Please understand that this does not mean that you should just allow your kids to wreck your house as much as they want. There are still certain boundaries on how much freedom you should let them have, especially if it would be dangerous for them. It is up to you how to draw this line. As long as they are safe and the surroundings are secure, it is better if you let them explore and handle things on their own.

Shield your kids from parental conflicts.

Kids learn how to communicate with others by copying how their parents get along with each other. It is very harmful for a child to be exposed to angry interactions between parents such as yelling and screaming, put downs, blaming, harsh criticisms, sarcastic remarks, and threats of harm and intimidation.

Parents should learn to restrain themselves and to control their emotions when kids are present. It's essential to avoid putting your children in the middle of your fights.

As parents, you should realize that exposing your children to your arguments and fights is a form of emotional abuse. Do not let yourself be the main culprit why your kids are having a hard time controlling their temper. Always practice patience, understanding, respect and love, especially with your spouse.

Make anger your ally.

Your kid's anger can give you a helpful insight about yourself and your parenting style. Sometimes, understanding your child's anger can help you better understand and heal your own angry past.

Is your child reacting in the same way you did as a child? Maybe you're doing the same things your own parents were doing that infuriated you when you were a kid. This is a good time to reflect about how you were treated when you were young and not do the same mistakes to your children again. It is good to know that your troubled past is still good for something, if only to improve your own parenting skills. Save your kids from the suffering you have experienced in the past by making things new and better for them.

If you were always reprimanded and scolded during childhood, try a different approach. Calmly tell your kids what you want them to do. Allow them to express their feelings, opinions or reasons why they are doing something the way it is and you would be surprised in knowing more about their personality. If you think that their reasons are not helpful, then talk it out with them. Kids do understand if you try to let them understand.

Chapter 3: Managing Kids' Anger about Divorce

Nobody usually really wants a divorce, but if it is inevitable, it pays to keep in mind how it affects your kids.

When parents get divorced, their children justifiably feel hurt at being let down by parents who are supposed to protect them from pain. They typically mask the pain with anger and aggressive behavior. Kids are normally conflicted in their emotions toward each of their parents. Some of these emotions include anger at one parent for leaving, fear that the other parent will leave too, and guilt over the belief that they somehow caused their parents separation.

Often, kids don't express their anger openly at their parents. Instead, they act out in school, fight with their siblings or lock themselves in their bedrooms.

The good news is that children are highly adaptive and resilient in nature and can cope with separation and divorce if you create opportunities to relieve the pain from their young hearts.

Divorce is understandably difficult for you and you may find it hard to have the energy to deal with your kids' anger issues. Start by taking care of yourself so you can be there for your kids. If you need to vent out your anger and frustration to a support group or a therapist so you don't take it out on your kids, do so.

The best thing you can do for your kids if you're undergoing a divorce is offer your presence, unconditional love and reassurance. Understand that your kids' anger and anxiety are normal reactions to this big change happening in their lives.

Taking care of yourself

Divorce can have a terrible effect on anyone, especially on the couples themselves who are about to undergo it. If you are going through this highly stressful ordeal, it is important to know how to take care of yourself first of all in order to be effective in making it easy for your children as well.

The first thing to do is to ensure that you are parting ways with your partner as gracefully as you can. Of course, this is easier said than done, but it is essential for you to move on and feel better much quicker.

A graceful separation will also help the both of you a lot for the long haul. Besides, the main reason of your divorce should always be to feel better than before. If it is not the case, then you should reconsider and re-assess your decision. The feeling should be mutual between you and your spouse so you can both move on freely with your own lives.

When you have established a common decision between the two of you, you will prevent feelings of guilt, shame, hatred, and bitterness toward each other. It is important that you both share the blame (if you want to call it that way) or the responsibility of being divorced, and not put everything on just one party. This will make you feel that you are actually doing the right thing.

Next is to focus on your health and wellbeing. Continue to eat the right kinds of food, have consistent daily exercise and most important of all, have adequate sleep and rest every day. You have to prioritize these things for your body to cope with the physical, mental and emotional stresses of going through a divorce.

Another effective way to handle a divorce is to find a support group. This could be your friends or a formal group within your community. The most common mistake of a recent divorcee is not asking for other people's support and help thinking that it is embarrassing or that they do not need it. More often than not, these people are also having a hard time moving on from a divorce.

The affirmation and encouragement that you get to receive from others is a major life changer. The positive effects of a social group for divorcees are actually highly documented. Moreover, being in a group could also help you become more accountable about your goals of getting back on your feet, dealing with your children and moving on happily with your life.

Lastly, always keep in mind the reason (or reasons) why you and your spouse decided to get divorced.

Remembering the *why* is important to keep you sane and confident. If you think that everything does not make sense, then again you should reconsider. There must be a big *why*, which makes it worthwhile to undergo all these suffering and changes.

If you are able to take care of yourself properly, then you are more than capable of taking care of your children as well. Read on and find out how to manage your kids' frustrations and anger about your divorce.

Listen to your kids

You may not be able to change your kids' feelings of sadness and frustration to happiness but acknowledging what they feel and encouraging them to express their sadness and frustration helps them make peace with the situation. Kids need to know someone cares enough to hear them out.

Don't dismiss whatever your kids have to say. Build trust by assuring them that they don't have to hold back in talking about their honest feelings. If you see that they have difficulty expressing themselves, help them find words for their feelings.

Help your kids to speak out and really pay attention to what they have to say. Do not just be there, but actually be there and listen. Let them know that there is nothing wrong with what they are feeling at the moment. You can even tell them that it is also very hard for you as the parent. Having open communication may not be the quick fix for this kind of problem, but it will make everything easier and lighter for your kids.

Clear up misunderstandings

Remind your kids as often as you need to that they are not responsible for the divorce. Explain to them why you decided to get a divorce without overwhelming them with the details. Hearing the real reason can help kids to understand. However, you need to choose carefully how much information to tell them. Older kids may need more details while younger kids do better with a simple explanation. Never provide details of the other parent's behavior or make your kids feel that they have to choose between you and the other parent.

Also set proper expectations to your kids about changes in their living arrangements, school and activities. More importantly, assure your kids that even though the physical circumstances of the family unit will change, both parents will always love them and will be there for them.

Watch out for signs of more serious problems

Expect that it will take some time for your kids to come to terms with the divorce or separation. However, if you don't see gradual improvement over several months, or behaviors become extreme, do your kids a favor and get professional help. Child therapists help hundreds or thousands of families go through this process and a good professional can be valuable in helping your kids cope and move on.

Here are some red flags that tell you your kids might need professional help:

Long periods of sadness

Trouble at school

Withdrawn behavior

Changes in daily habits

Frequent violent outbursts or temper tantrums

Poor concentration

Self-injury and eating disorders

Taking anger out to other children

Feeling anxious or worried

If these problems start suddenly after the divorce, are more extreme than you normally see in other children and last a long time, getting extra help is important.

Chapter 4: How Favoritism Provokes Kids to Anger

Playing favorites encourages high levels of anger and aggression within sibling relationships. When parents favor one child over another, the less-favored child carries around feelings of not being good enough which damages his self-worth. It also negatively affects the favored child who will soon feel the resentment of his siblings and can ultimately make him hate being the star child.

Aside from that, the favored child will also feel more pressure in the long run from his parents who have higher expectations in everything that he will do. Because of these different sets of expectations, the favored child may not find his own true personality, unlike the less-favored child who seems quite free to make mistakes and undertake risks in life because it is somewhat expected of him.

Whatever is the case, the major thing to realize is this: if you play favorites as a parent, you are actually putting all of your kids at a disadvantage, whether he or she is the favored or less-favored one.

Ways on How You Are Showing Favoritism

In fairness to the parents, most of the time they are actually not aware of favoring one child over the other. Maybe mom and dad are simply not sensitive enough or the circumstances just call for them to favor one over another. However, what if it becomes the case all of the time? Maybe the other kids will no longer perceive it as unintentional.

However, whether it is unintentional or not, that should not be an excuse to be negligent and just keep on favoring one child. Here are three classic ways on how you are showing favoritism in your family:

- Basing family decisions and actions around a specific child

  "We are all moving to Alaska!" you said. "Why mom?" Some of your children ask. "Because your brother wants to study there!" This is an obvious case of extreme favoritism. It is certainly not good to change the entire lives of your other children just to follow the preference of one of them.

  Another simple example is this: Sam has three sons who were all born in February, on the 8th, the 17th, and the 28th. They were born two years apart from one another. However, time and again when it comes to celebrating their birthdays, they only do so every 28th, which is the birthday of the eldest. This may just be a small thing for the parents and they may not actually deliberately favor the eldest child. However, for the other two sons, this kind of system may damage their self-esteem over the years.

- Giving out less severe punishments for the same misconduct or inappropriate behavior

  While fairness is not possible at all times, you should grant the same punishment for the same wrongdoing as much as you can. It may not be exactly the same, but the gravity or severity of reprimands should be at a consistent level. Administering harsher punishments for a specific child would tarnish his self-esteem for life. On the other hand, you are giving the favored child an unhealthy sense of entitlement by making giving him or her gentler punishments.

- Buying more material stuff for one specific child

  This is another common way of showing favoritism within the family. Although you cannot always monitor or buy the same kind of stuff for each of your children, it is better to become mindful of how much material possessions you are giving each one of them and no one should be obviously more privileged than the others.

Your kids tend to sense easily when you're playing favorites. You must guard against anything that would result in your children developing feelings of being "less worthy" than their siblings.

Try these ways to keep harmony and fairness in your home:

Do not compare siblings

A child being constantly told "Why can't you be like your brother/sister?" can develop lasting resentment, jealousy and low self-esteem. Statements of comparison can discourage a sibling from even trying because he feels like he could never keep up with his favored sibling.

Praising one kid's behavior in contrast to a sibling puts unfair pressure on the one you praised and belittles the other.

There are some parents who still use this outdated, ineffective "comparing and shaming" method in hopes of motivating his or her child to do something.

"Why can't you make your room nice and clean like your sister?"

"Why can't you brush your teeth properly like your sister?"

"Why can't you finish your homework on time like your sister?"

"Why can't you get high grades at school like your sister?"

And the comparisons go on and on from there. Surely, your child will hate his sister and hate you as well. If you keep on doing this, then he will grow up not wanting to try anything because he thinks that he is not good enough at anything to match up with his sister.

Also, never ever praise one of your children at the expense of the other, especially when the other one hears it. For example, do not say "Julia, you are so good at

Math! Not like your brother who still needs his toes to put together ten and ten!" You can just say, "Good job!" to compliment her and not hurt the feelings of anyone.

Do not take sides in a fight

One of the reasons why one sibling feels his mom or dad favors his brother or sister is when parents get involved in their quarrels. Unfortunately, parents tend to see one child as being in the wrong and punish that child while sparing the other.

While it is the role of the parents to try and pacify them, it is not good to explicitly show that one child is favored over the other in a sibling quarrel. If you can undoubtedly see that one is at fault and the other one is just a victim, do not go into a spanking spree right away. Explain what happened and let them understand what happened, and if ever what needs to be avoided in the future, before subjecting both of them to any form of punishment.

If you want to avoid showing favoritism, listen openly to all sides. After all, it takes two cooperating to make a fight. If you have to punish, punish both siblings equally. For example, if two siblings can't share the PlayStation without fighting, both don't get to play with it. If they bicker over who gets to wear the pink dress, neither of them could.

Listen to unfairness complaints when they arise

You don't have to drive yourself crazy trying to make it "fair" all the time. Sometimes your kids' "it's not fair" complaints arise from trying to manipulate you to give in to their wants. But sometimes, the complaining child is really asking for attention and approval from you that he is truly missing.

If you constantly practice fairness in treating your kids, then you can immediately refute the unfairness complaints. However, as just mentioned, it is not always possible to do that especially when you are trying to protect a particular child from something that you know would harm him or her. For sure, you know the capabilities and idiosyncrasies of each of your children, so you know how much they can handle things individually.

For example, one of your sons may be more adventurous than the other and is perfectly capable to ride a rollercoaster on his own. The other may be too shy or timid that he needs you to be with him on the ride. Explain to your more adventurous son how his brother needs you in a way that will make him feel compassionate and not jealous. You would be amazed at how even at such a young age, children easily understand these kinds of things.

Spend alone time with each child

Spending special alone time with each of your kids is an excellent way to make them feel treasured. It also gives you better insight into your child's unique traits and personality. It helps you figure out how you can be more responsive to your child.

Give each of your children your own individual time. This can be difficult if you have a big family, but all the hard work is surely going to be worth it. Ask your spouse to do the same as each one of your kids needs time alone with both of you separately.

The best antidote for favoritism is to favor all your children. It's critical that all children feel loved and highly prized for what makes them unique and special. Make them understand that they are all appreciated for their individuality and because of this, they don't need to compete with their siblings for your love and attention.

Chapter 5: Anger Triggered by the Pain of Rejection

Rejection hurts. It's one of the most distressing experiences in life. We are hardwired to react with anger and sadness when we are rejected or threatened with rejection. It's especially devastating for kids who thrive on feelings of recognition and acceptance. Feeling that he is not liked is enough to make a child's world collapse.

Children experience rejection in so many ways - being picked last for a basketball team, being called names, not being invited to a party, or being ignored deliberately by peers. Children who can't cope with rejection can misdirect resentment toward his siblings or his parents.

If your child's anger is triggered by being excluded and having a difficult time getting along with peers, help your child to move beyond this negative experience by being there to talk and listen to him, validate his feelings and navigate the struggles in his relationships.

Rejection at Home

There are many ways for children to experience rejection even right at their own homes. They may get it from their parents, siblings and other relatives, and this is perhaps the most painful and tragic way of feeling rejected. Studies show that kids who grew up in a home where they did not feel loved, protected, or valued are those who have the most social, emotional, and relational problems during their adulthood.

Most of the time, these feelings of rejection at home are induced by the parents themselves. If you are a parent, then it is extremely important for you to be careful with all the words that come out of your mouth in the presence of your children. Constant fighting and arguing between you and your spouse could damage a child's psyche and emotions for life.

When you often compare your child to other children, especially with their own siblings, it makes them feel inadequate and rejected. There are also some parents who inadvertently cry out expletives and other defaming words towards their children, like "You worthless piece of garbage!" or "Shut up and get out of here!" In the height of their anger and disappointment, they did not know that they themselves are the ones who are putting the emotions of their children in peril.

When a child is always compared, shouted at, spanked, and even ignored, he or she will not be able to get the necessary care and encouragement to build his own self-esteem. While it is most common for kids to find rejection outside the home, it is unfortunate that there are still those who suffer from it right at home. As parents, you should do your best not to sabotage your own child's self-esteem.

Sometimes, a child may experience rejection right after he or she was born. This is usually the case when parents are unwed, or not yet ready to have a baby, or when the pregnancy was unplanned and the mother was forced to continue with it. The mother or both parents may feel that the child is unwanted.

A fleeting thought of it is not really detrimental to a child, as sooner or later acceptance and joy may come to the parents. However, an intense and sustained feeling of regret by the parents will later on affect their treatment to the baby and the child will be able to feel it. Some researchers say that after the first trimester of pregnancy, the fetus in the womb could already feel this kind of rejection from the mother.

Rejection Outside the Home

Bullies at school or around the neighborhood are the usual culprits of rejection outside the home. There are children who act aggressively towards other children, singling them out or making fun of someone's disability or abnormality. Experts say that kids who behave this way are most likely bullied in their own homes as well, and they tend to retaliate to other kids who they think will allow them to.

Studies have shown that people who have experienced peer rejection during their childhood years are four times more probable to quit school by the tenth grade. They also tend to have low grades and fail in classes more often. Teachers also find them as loners, apprehensive, timid and always discouraged. What is worse is that children who suffer from recurrent peer rejection is more likely to abuse drugs and alcohol starting from their teenage years.

The self-esteem problems brought by peer rejection during childhood are definitely not a laughing matter. As parents, you should be able to do your best to safeguard your kids from it.

Help your child find his own ways of coping

However, you should not be overprotective or too controlling when it comes to raising your child. You should not be paranoid either. There is a perfect balance between safeguarding your child from bullies and allowing them to learn how to accept rejections and disappointments in life. As a parent, you must find that balance.

Do not jump in to save your child from every upsetting experience. Being over involved and overprotective only makes your child dependent on you and unable to bounce back from any rejection he may experience.

It is not your part to make your child's world disappointment-proof or rejection-proof. Your job is to teach your child how to cope with these eventualities in life. You can do so by gradually introducing to him or her ways on how he can handle them, and at the same time showing or modelling how it is done.

Support your child's independence by showing faith that he will recover from the sting of rejection. Every time your child overcomes challenges and setbacks, he actually grows stronger.

Be patient. It takes time to develop social skills and resilience to rise above rejections and challenges. Remember that your child's anger is just a symptom of a deeper disappointment. You focus is not to restrain anger but to build your child's confidence to help him get through rough times without exploding and hurting other people.

Help your child to realize that if he does not resolve his anger from a particular hurt, this anger can damage friendships and can limit participation in sports and other group activities.

Examine your child's behaviors that may push away friends

Everyone gets left out by friends from time to time and usually, they get over it. But if criticism and rejection happen to your child once too often, your child may be acting in ways that are off-putting to his peers. Here are some common behaviors that make it hard for your kids to be accepted by peers:

Bragging

Being oblivious to others reaction

Being a poor sport

Trying so hard to be funny

Ways to help your child improve social relationships:

> Instead of bragging to impress friends, discover with your child what he shares in common with peers and help him create ways to make friends with classmates with shared interests.

> Help your child pick up on social cues to stop a behaviour that annoys his peers. You may need to tell your child that a friend looking away or walking away can mean that he has lost interest in a topic and can be a sign to stop talking.

> Help your child build tolerance for losing in games by encouraging him to have fun playing games with friends win or lose.

> If you believe that your child is better off trying to be kind than funny, come up with possible opportunities for acts of kindness to try at school.

Help your kids accept unchangeable features in their lives

One of the challenges young children face is when they are ridiculed because of physical appearance, race, mental capabilities and family background. Being mocked as a person is a devastating blow to a child's self-esteem. This can cause the child to disown himself and feel shame for who he is.

Unless kids come to terms with it, these unchangeable features will remain as tension points that will continue to trigger bouts of anger while growing up.

It is important to reinforce the positive aspects of your child's appearance. Help your child embrace who he is. Get rid of the shame and clean out the "I am ugly", "I am bad", "I'm not worthy" belief implanted on your child's consciousness.

Chapter 6: Understanding Your Child's Temperament

While a child's angry behavior is usually triggered by frustrating events in his life, it may also be influenced by his own temperament. Your child is born with a preferred style of reacting to the world around him.

An important question you should be asking is "who is my child, and how can I be more responsive to the hand I've been dealt?" When you understand your child's temperament, you can work with him more easily in finding ways to improve his chance of successfully dealing with his emotions and life's challenges.

Many scientific studies have continued to show that temperament greatly influences kids' development. Observe how your kids react to each situation to gain insights of their behavioural tendencies.

By knowing the different traits of temperament, you will be able to understand your child better. It is important to keep in mind that each person is unique, and the same is true even for the children. There is no one who is exactly like the other, even identical twins.

The principles of child rearing may remain the same throughout the years, but the methods are ever changing, especially on how you will treat each particular child. This distinctiveness and individuality is also true even in siblings. If you have more than one child, then it is essential to realize that you may find a way to be as fair as possible, but you can't treat all of your children the same way every time. All of them have different needs, personalities and temperaments that you need to discover, which can make parenting interesting and a lot of fun as well.

Temperament Traits

These 9 temperament traits are developed based on a research conducted by Doctors Alexander Thomas and Stella Chess:

Activity Level: the extent of your child's motor activity. Is your child generally moving and doing something or is content to sit quietly and prefer activities not requiring much physical activities? Highly active kids need help in channelling their energy. This may be through dancing or sporty activities.

Adaptability: how your child adapts to changes in his environment. Does your child quickly adapt to new situations or does it take a long time to be comfortable with changes in routines? Slow-to-adapt kids need to know what's going to happen and usually need time to shift from one activity to another. They are not being stubborn, they're just cautious. And they need your support. On the other hand, kids who jump into things quickly need to be taught to think and then act before they find themselves in dangerous situations.

Persistence: your child's attention span and persistence in an activity. Does your child move on to another activity in the face of a tough challenge or does he continue to work on the activity until he gets it right? Persistent kids may be negatively labelled as stubborn because they usually persist in an activity even though they're asked to stop. Kids with low persistence may find it easier to develop strong social skills because they recognize that they can get help from other people.

Intensity: the energy level of responses whether positive or negative. Does your child react strongly to everything or tend to get quiet when upset? Intense kids need help in learning how to calm themselves. They may be quite exhausting to deal with because of the depth of their emotion. If you identify that your child's reaction can be intense, you may want to expose him in the dramatic arts.

Mood: your child's tendency to react to situations in a positive or negative way. Is your child generally happy or serious? Is he generally even-tempered or does his mood shift easily? Serious kids tend to carefully evaluate situations.

Regularity: the predictability of your child's biological functions like eating and sleeping. Does your child gets hungry or tired at predictable times or is somewhat irregular in his eating and sleeping habits? Regular kids need predictable routines while irregular kids need flexibility.

Distractibility: the degree of your child's concentration. How easily is your child distracted? Does he become sidetracked easily when working on some activity? It may be easier to divert an easily-distracted child from an undesirable behaviour. On the other hand, it may be difficult for him to finish an important assignment.

Sensory threshold: your child's sensitivity to physical stimuli. Does your child react positively or negatively to sounds, temperature, taste and touch? Sensitive kids are easily bothered by sensations.

Approach/Withdrawal: your child's response to a new object or person. Does your child accept a new experience or withdraws from it? Slow-to-warm up kids are resistant when faced with new things, people or situations. They are less likely to act impulsively.

Temperament Types

There are 3 basic types of temperaments formed by a combination of the 9 temperament traits: easy, difficult and slow to warm-up. Each child has his or her own pattern of temperament based on these three. Keep in mind, though, that these are just general classifications. These are just labels used to categorize certain behaviors and do not indicate the complete personality of a child.

The easy child is generally calm and in a positive mood. He quickly establishes regular routines and adapts easily to new environment. When he gets upset, he easily recovers and does so with only a little irritation or distress. As the name implies, it is easy for him to make new friends and some parents refer to him as "a good kid".

The easy child rarely demands attention. Because of this, it may be necessary for you to intentionally set aside special time to talk to your child about his pain, frustrations and struggles because he won't ask for it.

The difficult child tends to react negatively, engages in irregular habits, gets easily troubled by sensations, displays intense emotions and is fearful of new people and experiences. Some kids under this category may have a hard time adapting at school, and their presence may negatively affect teachers and classmates. For sure, difficult children are more challenging to raise and would require more of your wisdom and understanding to properly train him.

You may need to make a number of accommodations for your difficult child including providing opportunities that allow him to work off stored up energy, being flexible with setting up routines and indentifying the sensations that bother him.

The cautious or slow-to-warm up child has a low activity level, tends to withdraw, reacts negatively to new situations and displays low intensity of mood. But with continuous exposure, his reactions eventually become more positive.

He is slow to adapt to a new environment or new people. He is shy to meet unfamiliar people, which makes him slow to acquire new friends and may be perceived by teachers as a loner. He is passive, and when confronted with a problem or challenge, he tends to back away from it or become fearful and anxious. However, his reactions and responses will get better as he becomes more familiar with the same people and challenges.

Go slow on the cautious child. Allow him ample time to accept new situations and establish new relationships.

Adapting to your child's temperament

If you have determined your child's unique temperament, you also need to be aware of your own temperament traits and identify areas that conflict with your child. This way, you can make the first move to adapt and adjust your parenting methods in order to avoid clash of temperaments between you and your child.

When you understand your own temperament and your child's, you're not left in the dark. You can better understand the needs and emotions each of you is experiencing.

One very important thing to keep in mind is to accept and focus on the hand your holding not on what you wish your child should be. You may long for an easy child but you gave birth to a moody and inflexible child. You have to accept this reality and be a positive guide to your child's natural way of responding to his environment.

This way, it will not only be easier for your child, but will also be more convenient for you. Although raising a child can never be described as "easy", it is quite possible to do it more conveniently if you have the knowledge and skills to do it.

Goodness of Fit

The term "goodness of fit" refers to the appropriateness of a child's environment to his temperament. The environment is composed of the treatment he gets at home and outside of it, such as in the neighborhood or in school. When a child's environment is not healthy for him (meaning his temperament is always challenged and not catered), it is called "poorness of fit."

This concept is essential to help you assess the kind of environment you want to subject your child into. By knowing more and understanding how his or her own unique temperament works, you will be able to choose the right school and bring him to the right neighborhood friends he can hang around with in the community playground.

Another thing to keep in mind is that in a school environment, teachers most often relate well with easy children and difficult children, rather than the cautious or slow-to-warm up children. Obviously, easy children are easy to get along with, while difficult children tend to get the attention of teachers because of their aggressive behavior.

This leaves the cautious or slow-to-warm up children on the sidelines and because they are usually alone and quiet, people most often lean towards ignoring or overlooking them. If you think your child is under the cautious or slow-to-warm up category, you may want to talk to his teachers in school about his personality and temperament.

Goodness of fit may also refer to a child's ability to learn better in a certain method of teaching. Different children absorb knowledge and information in different ways, so how a teacher actually teaches kids is a consideration as well.

Conclusion

Thank you again for downloading this book!

Whether you're a parent puzzled about your child's anger and temperament or going through a major life change like divorce and want to be prepared to tackle your child's reactions, I hope the insights in this book benefited you personally. Here are some pointers to take with you:

Anger is an important part of life. Accept your child's anger and help him channel it to constructive ends. Help your child understand that feeling angry is normal but acting violently when angry can have negative consequences.

Unearth the story of your child's pain. Without this uncovering, anger can pile up for many years. Fixing the cause usually tames the anger.

Model appropriate expressions of anger. Remember, your child learns from your example.

Don't expose your child to conflicts between you and his other parent. Kids can develop resentment and bitterness in their lives as a result of parental conflict.

Know yourself and your child. This knowledge enables you to choose a more effective and sensitive response when confronted with your child's temper.

Your child is his own person. Understand that his temperament and personality are part of the unique qualities that make him special. Don't deny him a healthy self-esteem by expecting him to meet your preconceived notions of who he should be.

Be patient. Learning to channel anger in healthy ways takes time. In fact, many adults haven't mastered managing their anger either.

Be there to show affection. Kids are usually calmed by their parents' presence and warmth.

When you understand the nature of anger and deal with your angry child equipped with this understanding, you are improving his chance of living a happy and successful life. After all, just like happy emotions, unpleasant feelings of anger are vital in helping every one of us make sense of life's complexity and evaluate our experiences.

Do you like "How to Deal with Angry and Temperamental Kids"?

If you enjoyed this book, then I'd like to ask you for a favor, would you be kind enough to leave a review for this book on Amazon? It'd be greatly appreciated!

Leave a review for this book on Amazon by searching for title.

Thank you and good luck!

Check Out My Other Books

Below you'll find some of my other popular books that are popular on Amazon and Kindle as well. Simply click on the links below to check them out. Alternatively, you can visit my author page on Amazon to see other work done by me.

https://www.amazon.com/author/clairestranberg

50 Do-It-Yourself Household Hacks and Tips: Home Improvement Hacks at your Fingertips

The Remedy to Negativity: How to Deal with Pessimistic People and Cure Negative Emotions

The Ultimate Guide to Dog Training: Learn the Basic Ways to Train your Dogs and be your Dog's Bestfriend

Make Friends and Influence People: Know the Secrets to Getting More Friends and Influencing People

The Stage-Fright Cure: How to Overcome Stage-Fright and be the Best Public Speaker for Life

Leadership: A Practical Guide on Self-Development and How to be a Great Leader and Influence People

The Secrets to Memory Improvement: Boost your Memory and Improve Your Thinking Skills

The Child Who Loves to Read: How to Teach your Child to Love Reading at an Early Age

Beat Procrastination: A Concise Guide on How to Get Things Done Fast

Defeating Depression: How to Overcome Depression and Improve Your Quality of Life in 30 Days or Less

Sleep Apnea Cure: Find out the Cure to Sleep Apnea and You Will Sleep Soundly Every Night

Frugality is Everything: A Step-by-Step Guidebook in Managing your Finances Made Faster, Easier and Better Just for You

Asthma Relief Made Easy: How to Reduce Asthma Attacks Naturally

The Ultimate Guide to Speed Reading: How to Read Fast and Learn Quick

You can simply search for these titles on the Amazon website to find them.

Get an Awesome Gift Right Now!

Get your FREE GIFT NOW by going to

http://www.mritchi.com/free-ebooks/

As a way of saying thanks for your purchase, I'm offering these 2 books for FREE exclusive to my readers.

Also, you'll be the first to GET an instant access to FREE giveaways and freebies EXCLUSIVE to our SUBSCRIBERS only.

Get your FREE GIFT NOW by going to

http://www.mritchi.com/free-ebooks/

Printed in Great Britain
by Amazon